CHRIST IN THE WILDERNESS

CHRIST IN THE WILDERNESS

Reflecting on the paintings by Stanley Spencer

STEPHEN COTTRELL

First published in Great Britain in 2012

Society for Promoting Christian Knowledge
36 Causton Street
London SW1P 4ST
www.spckpublishing.co.uk

British Library Cataloguing-in-Publication Data
A catalogue record for this book is available from the British Library

ISBN 978–0–281–06208–9
eBook ISBN 978–0–281–06953–8

1 3 5 7 9 10 8 6 4 2

Typeset by Caroline Waldron, Wirral, Cheshire
Printed in Great Britain by 4edge Limited

eBook by Graphicraft Limited, Hong Kong

Produced on paper from sustainable forests

For Rebecca

I like to go beachcombing, and I like to find interestingly shaped rocks. When I really get into the groove I start finding beautiful rocks everywhere, until I discover that all the rocks on the beach are beautiful. And so I try to find beauty in even the smallest moments, because beauty is something that can grow if you let it.

Douglas Coupland, interview at the back of *Eleanor Rigby*,
Harper Perennial, 2005, p. 8

I was disturbed by feelings of everything being meaningless. But quite suddenly I became aware that everything was full of special meaning and this made everything holy.

Stanley Spencer, *Sermons by Artists*,
Golden Cockerel Press, 1934, p. 50

Contents

Illustrations

Acknowledgements

Most of the reflections in this book come from my own meditations on the pictures themselves. Although a lot has been written about Stanley Spencer, not that much has been written about these particular paintings. I am, however, very grateful to Richard Harries, one-time Bishop of Oxford, for letting me see and quote the notes that he prepared on these paintings. I worked with Richard for a few years when I was Bishop of Reading and I learned of his love for Stanley Spencer and his great knowledge of Spencer's paintings. I am also grateful for the support of the Stanley Spencer Gallery in Cookham. I spent a happy day looking through their archive, where I was able to unearth various bits and pieces which have helped flesh out this book, not least my discovery of the sermon Stanley Spencer himself wrote, which was published in 1934, and then of Richard Harries' sermon preached on the 100th anniversary of Spencer's birth. Ann Danks, the archivist in Cookham, very kindly sent me copies of the notes about the paintings that Spencer dictated to his niece, Daphne, in 1950, and the photographs of the paintings in Cookham church. She and others at the gallery, where I had the great privilege of preaching at the service to mark its 50th anniversary in 2012, have enthusiastically supported the writing of this book. Charles Miller, the Rector of Abingdon, has also written frequently with notes and encouragement.

Acknowledgements

As I say in the book, I have spoken about these paintings on numerous occasions. I therefore wish to thank the many individuals whose own observations and insights given in the course of a hundred presentations have contributed to this book, not least much loved colleagues Angela Butler, Martin Cavender, James Lawrence, Robert Warren and Alison White, who have heard me speak about them many, many times. I particularly remember clergy conferences, travelling schools, retreats and parish weekends with churches from Todmorden, Cholsey and Saffron Walden; a families camp at Hilfield Friary; a retreat at Los Olivos, near Granada in southern Spain; and lectures given in Reading and at the Sandham Memorial Chapel in Burghclere, where Amanda Findlay, the curator, offered fantastic support for this project.

Finally, I need to thank Joanna Moriarty and Lauren Zimmerman at SPCK. Joanna commissioned the book, thus giving me the opportunity to write the book I have been dreaming about for years. She was forbearing and patient as my move to become Bishop of Chelmsford rather delayed the delivery of the text. Lauren's editorial comments have improved and refined the writing. But this book has been a joy to write. Looking at these paintings has helped me to understand my own vocation to follow Christ. I hope it may do the same for all who read this book.

Introduction

Stanley Spencer and me

I only got three O levels. At my school – a not very high-flying boys' secondary modern in Essex – you needed five to swap to the grammar school, where they had a proper sixth form so you could take A levels and try for university. The choice at my school was either leave and get a job, or stay another year, sit some more O levels and maybe get a slightly better job. But there was not much expectation of anything else.

Inside, I knew I was capable of more, but I had dreamed, played and misbehaved my way through the previous five years, so I wasn't sure what I needed to do to make something else happen.

Next door to the boys' school was at the time a much better girls' school. Every school, whatever its label, is only as good as its teachers, and the girls, with excellent teachers and high expectations, were achieving much more than we were.

I can't remember who hatched the scheme, but one of my friends came up with the idea that we might join the sixth form in the girls' school and take some A levels there. Somehow this was agreed to, and each morning three of us registered in the boys' school and then joined the girls next door for all our lessons. Late in the day, my education had begun.

No human being can thrive without affirmation – this is one of the truths that the paintings in this book, and the Scriptures that lie behind them, reveal. In the sixth form at the girls' school I found teachers who believed in me. They did not think that education was about pouring knowledge in; rather, it was about drawing potential out. They opened my mind to many things, and opened doors to new learning and new possibilities. But most of all it was the affirmation they gave me, and the expectation that I could do well, which changed me.

I did three A levels, in the same subjects that I had got at O level previously – art, English and history. My English teacher, Mrs Bareham, spotted something in me and encouraged me to write. (Actually, I was already writing a huge amount; it was just that nobody had shown much interest before.) My art teacher was Rosemary Murray. She was a wonderfully zestful, disciplined, good-humoured radical. She sent us to life drawing classes at the local art college. She took us to galleries in London. She bought prints by contemporary artists to hang in the school (which must be worth quite a bit of money now; I hope the school knows what's under its nose!). And she introduced me to painters and artists I have come to love. One of them was Stanley Spencer.

I remember in one of our first lessons she showed us a copy of Spencer's early painting, *Swan Upping at Cookham*. I liked it immediately, though I didn't know why.

The paintings that we are looking at in this book are all by Stanley Spencer. He made his name around the time of the First World War. If you want to see some of the most remarkable examples of his paintings, go to the Sandham Memorial Chapel[1] at Burghclere, just off the A34, south of Newbury. It is an English Sistine chapel – only more glorious! The panels on either side of the chapel tell the story of Spencer's war experiences as an orderly, a stretcher bearer and, latterly, as an infantryman with the Berkshire Rifles. At the east end of the chapel is one of the most astonishing paintings of the twentieth century: *Resurrection of the Soldiers*, the first of several vast paintings where Spencer portrays the great Christian promise of the resurrection.

Spencer is probably best remembered for the many paintings in which he relocated the Christian story to his beloved village of Cookham. This picturesque Thames-side village in Berkshire was where Spencer was born, where he lived for the great majority of his life, and where he died. His most famous painting, which can sometimes be seen in Tate Britain in London, is again of the resurrection, but this time it is taking place in Cookham churchyard.

There are paintings of Christ carrying his cross up Cookham High Street, sharing a last supper in Cookham malthouse, and preaching at Cookham regatta. There is a marvellous little gem of a gallery in Cookham where his paintings and other memorabilia connected with his life can be seen.[2] He is, without doubt, one of the most important figures in twentieth-century English painting.

*

Of course, I didn't know any of this, nor the intense spiritual reality that Spencer located in everyday events, like swans being carried up the High Street, when, aged about 16, I saw the painting of swan upping for the first time. What appealed to me about it was its boldness, and the strange and satisfying patterns that Spencer saw between the outstretched necks of the swans and the arms of the men carrying the boats. I liked the way we looked down upon the scene. I was intrigued by a woman who stood on the bridge over the river, looking away from the action into a distance that we couldn't see. So began a life-long love of Spencer's paintings. Having seen them 'in the flesh' at the Tate Gallery, from then I started looking around for opportunities to see some more.

Thus it was that in 1991 – the centenary of Spencer's birth – I went to the impressive retrospective exhibition of Spencer's work at the Barbican Gallery in London, entitled *The Apotheosis of Love*. This celebration of his work tried to bring together as many of Spencer's religious paintings as possible in an attempt to create a display that echoed the various plans that Spencer drew up for what he called his 'Church House'. Having completed his work at the Sandham Memorial Chapel and enjoyed the enormous critical acclaim that followed, Spencer now began to conceive other grand and ambitious plans. Throughout his life he cherished in particular a dream of one great architectural scheme where all his paintings were brought together. Jane Alison observes:

> The Church-House dream fuses all of Spencer's preoccupations in an attempt to find a meaningful synthesis of the numinous and the secular, the desiring body and spiritual yearning. Spencer hoped that through the Church-House innocence and experience would be bridged; redemption and spiritual harmony attained.[3]

He imagined a building of many different rooms, with each one devoted to a particular subject, some specifically Christian, such as the Last Day (for Spencer not a day of judgement, but of joyful resurrection), and others, while still spiritual, more obviously human, such as a room focusing on the love mothers have for their children. The plan of the building was both like a church, with a nave and sanctuary and side aisles, and also like Cookham, reflecting the topography of the village. The nave would also be the High Street, with the transepts representing the crossroads at the top of the village; some of the chapels would be the homes of individuals he knew and loved; a side aisle would correspond to the river, and so on.

Spencer never found a patron for this grand project. Consequently landscapes and commissioned portraits became the bread-and-butter paintings that kept body and soul together. He referred to these disparagingly as his 'pot boilers'. Actually, the landscapes are beautiful evocations of the ordered beauty of the English countryside. And because he believed that even the tiniest little thing could bear the imprint of God and therefore the majesty of the whole, each petal of each daisy is lovingly rendered. As Alexandra Harris observes, 'he wanted to paint it all with the worshipful attentiveness of the Pre-Raphaelite, recording every fallen leaf and every blade of grass'.[4] Nevertheless, throughout his life he held on to the hope that this Church House project might one day come into being. It never did.

The genius of the Barbican exhibition was that as far as possible it arranged the paintings within the gallery according to the plans that Spencer himself had envisaged.

One of the rooms contained eight astonishing paintings. It was the Christ in the Wilderness room. Each one was a portrait of Christ: there was Christ praying in the morning, Christ delighting in the flowers of the field, and Christ observing the animals he encounters. None of them appeared to relate directly to the biblical account of the devil tempting Jesus in the wilderness. But they seemed to be describing all the other days that led up to this. 'He was with the wild beasts,' says St Mark's Gospel (Mark 1.13). I found myself encountering a sometimes solitary, sometimes mournful, sometimes inquisitive Jesus, at home in the wilderness – which in some of the pictures is lushly fertile – yet at the same time far from home in a wilderness that can be stark and forbidding.

Spencer's great biographer Kenneth Pople makes the observation that 'Stanley's Christ is a workmanlike figure fashioned in the image of the medieval master-masons he so admired . . . a powerful stubble bearded Christ quite unlike the conventional Victorian "pale Galilean".'[5] He concludes that Spencer has the ability, one which is so strange to the modern way of looking at things, of 'metamorphosing intense spiritual feeling into galaxies of associations which are given expression in direct and lucid images'.[6] This is certainly true of these pictures, which are some of Spencer's greatest paintings, and among the most important images of Christ produced in the last century.

*

Spencer's intentions for how the paintings should be viewed are a little confused. Speaking to his niece Daphne in 1950, he says how he often used to look up at the square panels in the ceiling of the chancel of Cookham church and wish that he could fill them all in some way.[7] He goes on:

> I suddenly seemed to tumble to the idea of trying to do the life of Christ in the Wilderness. I felt that because

you have not anything much in the actual life in the wilderness except the temptation, that one has an excuse for imagining what his life might have been like. And I rather liked the idea of Christ and Nature – simply. That so to speak, he gives a sort of preliminary 'once over' to that particular aspect of his creation. It seemed very peaceful and it seemed a thing that, humanly, one would wish to do before entering some big life mission. In each of the squares one would have had Christ with his surroundings and something indicating his relationship with it. Just as you would have God creating Adam, so you might have Christ looking into a tree and seeing the birds' nests – a sort of 'check over'. In order to get some kind of 'slant', as one might say on what, actually, he might have been doing all those 40 days and 40 nights.[8]

He originally intended to create 40 paintings in the series, and there are indeed 40 panels in the chancel roof of Cookham Parish Church. His paintings correspond precisely in size to the panels, so this desire to fill them seems a likely explanation. If correct, it also means that Spencer imagined us seeing all 40 pictures at once, and from below.

But on another occasion Spencer said this:

In doing these paintings of *Christ in the Wilderness* it was my wish that they should have been seen separately:

one for, and on, each day of Lent. I thought that if a little shrine or frame could have been made, so that each of these same-sized canvasses could be placed in it and removed from it each day, that like a calendar, the changing every day of these paintings of Christ's 40 days' and 40 nights' fast would help a person during Lent. In these works I have regarded Christ's dwelling in the Wilderness as a prelude forming part of the Ministry (or an introduction of considerable duration). Except for the last days when he was tempted, I don't know of any statements, which refer directly to his life during this period except the reference to his fasting. But there is evidence of an appreciation of nature and nature's ways in all his sayings . . . That being so, I have tried to visualise the being he is, and the life he lived from day to day using the sayings as a clue and guide.[9]

Whether he intended the paintings to be in the ceiling of the chancel of his Church House, or whether they were to be displayed one at a time and changed like a Lenten calendar, we do not know for sure. Knowing Spencer, he probably couldn't make his mind up. But certain things about the pictures are clear. His starting point for each one was Scripture. In one of his many journals and jottings, he records the fact that he is going to 'use Jesus' own utterances'[10] for the beginning of each picture. What Spencer is imagining is that each of the 40 paintings would represent one of Jesus' days in the wilderness.

It is not insignificant that Spencer completed most of these pictures – he only ever finished the eight that were displayed at the Barbican exhibition – during the first months of the Second World War, a time when the whole world was being stripped back and Europe found itself flung into a wilderness. He was also away from Cookham, separated from his beloved wife Hilda, entangled with another woman, and reeling somewhat from the downturn in his reputation caused by the explicitly erotic paintings he had recently produced. It was a most turbulent time in his life; it felt like being in a wilderness. Spencer associates himself closely with Christ. He dwells and meditates on Christ's 40 days of fasting in the wilderness. Consequently, the landscapes that Christ inhabits no longer resemble the Cookham he loves, though in one of the paintings – *Consider the Lilies* – we can probably make out the water meadows by the Thames that Spencer knew so well. Rather, these paintings show the rough terrain of a battle-scarred Macedonia, where he had served in the First World War; and the feelings of the paintings, despite their delight in creation, are similarly concerned with some of the harsh realities of privation and exile.

He is also reaching back inside himself. In these paintings 'he has gone back to the wonder of his early memory-feelings and is, in maturity, reproducing them'.[11] With the reassurance that the biblical texts give him, he sees again an affinity between his love of nature and Christ's closeness to the creation. In some of the writings held in the Tate Archive, Spencer says this:

In Christ, God beholds his creation, and this time has a mysterious occasion to associate himself with it. In this visitation, he contemplates the many familiar humble objects and places: the declivities, holes, pit-banks, boulders, rocks, hills, fields, ditches and so on. The thought of Christ considering all these seems to me to fulfil and consummate the life-wishes and meaning of all these things.[12]

In other words, Spencer saw Christ's contemplation of the creation as the creation's meaning: that it is God's greatest wish and desire that he should be known by all created things. God desires that the whole creation, from the tiniest pebble to the mightiest person, should sing in praise. As Jesus himself retorted, when the Pharisees told him to silence the crowds at his triumphant entry into Jerusalem, 'If these were silent, the stones would shout out' (Luke 19.40).

In this way Christ's sojourn in the wilderness – which is both exile and pilgrimage – is a time of preparation for all that follows. Christ's ministry is to draw all people and all creation into relationship with God, a relationship of wonder, love and praise.

*

Although Spencer made sketches for the whole series, only eight were completed, and there is a ninth half-finished picture.

Unfortunately, none of these can be seen in the UK, though one or two have become well-known images (*Rising from Sleep in the Morning*, for example, was on the cover of H. A. Williams' influential book *True Wilderness*). If you want to see the originals you will have to travel to the Art Gallery of Western Australia in Perth.

The paintings made a huge impact on me when I saw them. I bought the catalogue of the exhibition. I made slides of the paintings and I used them as illustrations for talks I gave at conferences, retreats and study days. They started out as the basis for simple meditative reflections for the end of a session. But the reflections got longer and soon the paintings, and what they said to me, became the talk! Consequently, this book has been writing itself in my head for over 20 years! However, every time I turn back to the paintings I find something new.

The paintings are about vocation. The wilderness is the place where Christ goes to refine and discover what it means for him to be God's suffering servant. They are, of course, also about Spencer's vocation as an artist who reveals the presence and pattern of God in everyday things. The themes of the paintings – the desert as a place of encounter and discovery; the fecundity of the wilderness and Christ's affinity with and love for the creation; the vivid portrayal of Christ's humanity; his brooding upon his calling – seem to me to speak cogently and powerfully to the longing that is prevalent in the world today for a deep, holistic and human spirituality.

It has been difficult to choose which pictures to write about and which ones to omit. The first painting in the series is not reproduced here. Taking its title from Mark 1.12, it is called *Driven by the Spirit into the Wilderness*. It is a powerful picture. An almost Tarzan-like Jesus strides across the rugged terrain of the wilderness, reaching out to the branches of trees for support. It is a scene setter, and worth mentioning here for the important reason that the Bible makes clear that Jesus' going into the desert is the work of the Holy Spirit. Whatever he will discover and whatever will happen to him there are part of the leading and directing of God.

But how does Spencer depict the driving force of the Spirit? The Hebrew word for spirit, *ruach*, also means 'wind', so one way to do this might have been to show the figure of Christ being propelled by a gale-force wind into the desert. But in this picture the trees are still. Neither are Christ's hair and his cloak blown about. Yet we see him reaching out to hold on to a branch to steady himself, as though he is feeling a great force. Richard Harries makes this important observation:

> There is an inner gale. His eyes look up and ahead towards a distant horizon. When blown by a great wind we grab anything, even brittle twigs as Christ does here. And we plant our feet firmly on the ground legs apart as here. Yet the landscape remains still. Christ is driven by an inner force.[13]

This inner force and where it leads is the subject matter of the rest of the paintings.

Spencer notes that as he was painting this picture, and the others in the series, he was thinking of Macedonia, where he had served in the First World War. At this time more than any other he knew the gnawing attrition of fear, which for him was not just the horror of war itself, but also what he described as 'the personal terror of being cut off from home life'.[14]

The other paintings not discussed here are *He Departed into a Mountain to Pray* and *The Eagles*. They are both powerfully beautiful. In the first, Jesus kneels in prayer before a great altar-like stone. Or perhaps it is like the edge of a bed? Although it is a mountain-top picture it speaks of the simple disciplines of prayer. His hands are together. He is saying his prayers as a child might. There is also a sense that the 'indoors' of the church is now 'outdoors' in the world. This is a theme of all the paintings: the earth is the place for encounter with God.

The Eagles is a violent and complex picture. Although Spencer, like many of us, could be horrified by the violence of nature, he was also impressed by its forcefulness, and does not shrink from showing its darker side. Based upon Jesus' saying, 'Wherever the corpse is, there the vultures [or the eagles] will gather' (Matthew 24.28; Luke 17.37), it is about the last things and the coming of the Son of Man. Three eagles have killed and are devouring an animal, some sort of gazelle. Jesus lies next to the killing, but he looks away. He makes no judgement on what is happening. After all, the eagles are only doing what eagles do. But one can't help but be reminded of the great promise in Isaiah, where the prophet speaks of a day when 'the wolf shall live with the lamb, the leopard shall lie down with the kid . . . they will not hurt or destroy on all my holy mountain' (Isaiah 11.6, 9). The painting seems to be about Christ's longing for a new creation, and his acceptance, but not necessarily his approval, of the horrors of this world as it is. Yes, nature is very beautiful, but it can also be cruel and desperately hard.

The paintings that we will be looking at portray a profound meditation on the disciplines and delights of prayer, and in *The Scorpion* an even deeper and darker meditation on death and Christ's own acceptance of his vocation to be the one who dies, the one who shares in the sufferings of the world.

*

To look at these paintings is itself an invitation to enter the desert through the doorway of your imagination. As Rowan Williams points out, 'a desert is an unpopulated place, and if we are to let God give what God wants to give we must somehow find that unpopulated place in ourselves'.[15] We therefore need to approach these pictures, and the reading of this book, with a certain openness: we need to allow ourselves to be surprised and disturbed. We need to be what Christ calls 'poor in spirit', less reliant on our own good ideas or intentions, and allow ourselves to be led by the Spirit of God. We need to cultivate a desire for stillness.

This is where pictures can help. To look at a picture – any picture – requires us to stop. A glance is not enough. And what we see here is a Christ who himself stops and looks. In every picture we will find Christ gazing: either intently up to God or with loving fascination and regard for God's creation in all its beauty and terror. Looking at these pictures carefully and deeply can be an antidote to the busyness of the modern mind. We are, after all, too used to endlessly changing, fast-moving and flickering images. Televisions, computers and iPads have affected the way we receive and regard images. We are always itching for the next one, searching for something else, flicking from channel to channel or satiated by the Google click which in a half a second delivers thousands. In these pictures we need to do the moving. Not the quick fleeting look, which then seeks out the next one to replace it, but a deep interior searching. We need to enter into the stillness and depth of the image and let it speak to us slowly. This little privation – staying with one image rather than fussing after more – may itself be a desert: a small self-denial that can bring great reward.

No one owns a desert. It isn't anyone's property. We come to it to be alone and to place ourselves in the presence of God. We may be 'owned' or 'possessed' by all sorts of things – our anxieties, our ambitions, our agendas, our fantasies, our lust for more – and we can all too easily consume ourselves with worry trying to defend or promote our own cause. But in the desert we are put back in touch with raw and basic necessities. We are, with Jesus, between the animals and the angels, between the basics of heaven and the basics of earth.

'The journey into the desert', says Williams, 'is a journey into a particular kind of spaciousness.'[16] This is the paradox of the desert that Jesus experiences. The bare emptiness of the desert is also a place of expansive discovery. In finding ways of living where the necessities of life are all we have, we are drawn deeper into an appreciation of God's goodness and provision. For without God there is nothing. It is the same paradox – the desert as encounter – that drew other seekers after God into lonely and desolate places. It is at the heart of these paintings. In the desert Jesus is simply a human being before God. Spencer depicts this beautifully. But he is also God entering into the beauty and mystery of his own creation. Entering into the world of these pictures can give us something of this experience. It can certainly tell the story. Through Spencer's deep meditations upon Christ's dwelling in the wilderness we can come to the wilderness too. We can find ourselves there, and we can find Christ.

The paintings on display in Cookham Parish Church in the 1950s

John Neal, Stanley Spencer Gallery, Cookham

The paintings on display in Cookham Parish Church in the 1950s

John Neal, Stanley Spencer Gallery, Cookham

So before you read each chapter, spend some time looking at the picture. Resist the temptation to begin reading immediately. Simply gather together and acknowledge your own responses to the picture before finding out what I have to say. Your reflections are just as important as mine. You may even want to jot some of them down. Spend some time puzzling over the passages of Scripture that Spencer chose as the starting point for each painting. It was these Scriptures, and his love of Scripture, that led Spencer to these particular images and to this revelation of the spaciousness of the desert as a place of refining fire and astonishing discovery.

*

Between 2004 and 2010 I had the great privilege of serving as the Bishop of Reading in the diocese of Oxford. Being Bishop of Reading essentially meant that I was Bishop of Berkshire, and so this also meant Bishop of Cookham. I found it moving to lead worship in Cookham church; to visit the place in the churchyard where Stanley Spencer's ashes are buried and the beautifully restored and re-ordered Stanley Spencer gallery; to walk by that bit of the River Thames that Spencer knew so well. Sometimes when I was celebrating the Eucharist I would look up to the chancel ceiling and imagine these paintings looking down at me.

During the 1950s these paintings were temporarily displayed in Cookham church (see pages 20–3). It must have delighted Spencer to see them in the church he loved so much. I hope you may also have such delight as you read this book and allow the story of these paintings to lead you with Christ into a wilderness of discovery and encounter.

1

Rising from Sleep in the Morning

Christ in the Wilderness: Rising from Sleep in the Morning (1940)

I don't find praying easy. On the one hand I truly believe that it is the most important thing I do each day. On the other hand, finding the discipline to match the desire is never as straightforward as I would like it to be. This is especially true when I am left to my own devices. There always seem to be good reasons to put off praying, or, when I do set time aside, my mind wanders, or I gallop through words that should be taken slowly, gulp down without chewing what needs to be savoured. I long for the intimacy and focus of prayer I see in this picture. Because for Jesus, prayer seems, for the most part, to have been joy. What we see here is not some solemn obligation or duty that has to be got through, but the delight of coming into the presence of the Father. The whole of Jesus' body is directed upwards to God, like an arrow pointing to the heavens.

Unlike some of the other pictures in this series, it is not possible to be sure which passage of Scripture Spencer had in mind when he painted this image of Jesus. There are several possibilities. In the Gospels Jesus often disappears, both to get away from the crowds (and his own disciples!) and to spend time with God. Indeed, it is this closeness to God that is most startling about his ministry. He is the one who calls God 'Father'.

Sometimes today people understandably have difficulty with the almost exclusively male language that the Bible uses to describe God. But there are exceptions, and one of them is the last picture we will look at in this series. However, we cannot avoid the intimacy of the language Jesus uses. In fact the Aramaic word that Jesus uses – *Abba* – is much more like the child-like 'Daddy', in contrast with some of the rather sterner connotations that the English translation 'Father' might suggest (see Mark 14.36, Mark's account of the Gethsemane story, where Jesus calls God Abba). This tenderness towards God was shocking to those who heard him, as it can still be shocking for us today. And even if you are one of those people who have had bad experiences of fathers, I hope that Jesus' revelation of God as the loving parent, the one in whom we can enjoy intimacy and communion, can be received as a precious gift to release us from the harder, more limiting patriarchal images that distort the radical simplicity of what Jesus was actually teaching.

What we see in this picture is a child delighting in the presence of the one in whom he is able to be completely himself. This is what a relationship of absolute love and trust gives us. We are set free to be ourselves; and even if life has never afforded us this sort of relationship, then it is on offer through that relationship with God that Jesus is making possible. Can we begin to discern in this picture the tiny child whose hands reach up in delight when its mother enters the room?

We may also note that right at the beginning of the Gospel story, as Jesus' ministry commences and he submits to John's baptism as a sign of his solidarity with all of sinful, broken humanity, the voice of God speaks from heaven to proclaim that this Christ, this man from Galilee who to all intents and purposes seems like any other man, is actually the Son of God: God entering the creation he has made; and not only a son, but a beloved one, in whom God is well pleased (see Mark 1.9–11). Many New Testament commentators have observed that this great affirmation of the Father's pleasure is the dynamic out of which Jesus' whole ministry flows. He knows that he is the beloved of God. He never doubts it; and even when the going gets very tough indeed, and he longs for there to be another way, he is still rooted in this relationship of trust and love.

It is a relationship that sustains him. It is a relationship that he turns to every day. In the very first chapter of Mark's Gospel, following a day of intense and fruitful ministry, we also read this: 'In the morning, while it was still very dark, he got up and went out to a deserted place, and there he prayed' (Mark 1.35). Since this verse speaks of a deserted place it already recalls the wilderness. It is therefore most likely that this was the piece of Scripture Spencer had in front of him when he began this painting. If this was the case, it is interesting that this passage not only tells us of Jesus' great desire to spend time with the Father, it also illustrates the fruitfulness of a prayerful life, for we are told in Mark 1.36 that 'Simon and his companions hunted for him'. There are clearly still people in Capernaum, where Jesus was ministering the day before, who need his presence: 'Everyone is looking for you,' Simon says (Mark 1.37). But astonishingly Jesus turns his back on these needs. He says no to Simon's request. 'Let us go on to the neighbouring towns,' says Jesus, 'so that I may proclaim the message there also; for that is what I came to do' (Mark 1.38). Somehow the intense focus of Jesus' prayer has created within him a clarity of purpose and a conviction about what must be done and what must be left undone. This is not itself the purpose of prayer, but it is the fruit of a prayerful life.

There is an alignment between the will of God and Jesus' own will. We should not think of this as easy or obvious (saying to ourselves that because he is God's son then of course he knew God's will). As we shall explore in a later chapter, the wilderness is for Jesus a place of encounter and temptation. Who Jesus is as God is contained and coterminous with what he is as a man; therefore he knows choice and with choice temptation, just as we do. In Gethsemane he pleads with God that other choices might prevail. Here it would have been possible to please both Simon and the crowds, and do the obvious thing and go back to Capernaum. But Jesus is in touch with a higher agenda, a compelling sense of God's call upon him and knowledge of God's choice in that situation. This knowledge was not something that came to him automatically, however. It had to be worked at, discovered and discerned. Therefore he rises early each morning, and he seeks out the wilderness, the place where everything is stripped back, in order that he might find communion with God and seek God's will.

Consequently, you can see that Spencer has painted Jesus in an intensely focused posture. His eyes stare towards heaven. His hands reach upwards in a gesture that combines praise and longing. He is reaching out to receive. He is pointing his whole body towards God.

There are different ways of reading all these paintings. Here Jesus is in what appears to be a crater. It is almost as if he is a missile about to blast off. Just as the Spirit drove him into the wilderness, now he is himself about to be propelled to God. Or, some people see his posture as being like a church spire, pointing to the heavens.

Most people observe that Jesus looks rather as if he could be a flower. As far as we know this was in fact Spencer's intention, although it may have been, even for him, a subconscious one, since it was only later that he made the connection. Speaking about the paintings years after they were finished, he said, 'I think I was, perhaps thinking of a flower opening.'[1] He also said:

> Christ liked to feel the fact that he was a man and that he might do a lot of the normal things that a human might do, such as going to bed and getting up in the morning: that it would be a very wonderful experience – that it would be, so to speak, the first getting up of a human being – almost like a rehearsal of the act – that the joy would consist in the waking and the awareness of his great lover 'God'.[2]

This shows how Spencer liked to see Christ living out God's delight in the creation. Remembering his wartime experiences in Macedonia, Spencer also notes that the crater Jesus rises from is like a shell-hole.

In this reading of the picture Jesus' arms reach upwards like the stamen of a flower and his robes are splayed out around him like the petals. This is what prayer is like, the painting seems to be saying. It is normal. It is natural. Just as a flower opens its leaves and its petals to the sun on a new day, so Jesus rises from sleep to pray.

Prayer won't always feel normal, it won't always feel natural – and that has certainly been my experience – and yet it should be, for we human beings are made for community with God. It is for this sort of intimacy with God that we are intended. Therefore our restless hearts will only find true rest and true peace when they allow themselves to be embraced by this communion with God.

And why does a plant open its leaves and petals to the sun on a new day? Well, it is part of that process whereby a plant creates energy for life. The leaves receive the energy of the sun. The brightly coloured petals attract. Although this is also true for prayer – when we pray we receive the energy we need for living – it is not the reason we pray.

The purpose of prayer is praise: not because God needs our thanks, but because without God there is nothing. Once we catch a glimpse of who God is, and realize the fact that each breath we take is a gift from God, then what can we do but pour out our thanks at the amazing miracle that life itself exists at all; within the precious oasis of this mysteriously beautiful planet, conscious life can reflect upon the fact of existence, and cry out in wonder and amazement. Prayer, then, is simply our stumbling thanks for all that God has already done. That we are here at all is amazing. That we are able to reflect upon our existence is miraculous, and made even more astonishing the more we learn from science about the fragile equilibrium of the universe and our own delicate part within it. How could we not give thanks?

But if there is a God who has made us, and who loves this creation and has a special care for us, not only as part of the creation but as the one part that is able to return praise (as far as we know), then the voice of our thanksgiving must soon turn to silence. For if in prayer we can know and give thanks to God, then we can also receive from God. Our minds and hearts can be fed and replenished; we can begin to know God's mind; there can be alignment between our own wills and the will of God. This sort of prayer has several names. It can begin as contemplation: simply resting in the presence of God and quietly giving thanks for who God is and the gifts of life we have received. But it can move to a more active meditation, where we ask God that we might know God's purposes for our lives and for the world. This focused receiving from God is what we see in this picture. If Jesus is painted as a flower, then this might be a lotus flower. In Tibetan Buddhism this flower is a symbol of prayer, particularly connected with purification of body, speech and mind, and the full blossoming of wholesome deeds. I don't know whether Spencer had such a parallel in mind, but within the Christian tradition, and brilliantly captured in this remarkable painting, prayer is portrayed as the vital defining characteristic of Jesus' life and ministry. It is reasonable to conjecture that this was something Jesus was schooled in before his ministry began. He broods upon the Scriptures. He attends to the worship of the synagogue. He gives himself to places of receiving. This is what the flower is doing.

However, as I look again at the painting I am also reminded of bindweed, whose white, bell-shaped flowers we used to call, as children, 'granny pop out of beds'. The flowers have a remarkable playfulness – when you pinch the head of its stem the flower jumps forth, as if propelled to the heavens.

Whatever flower you see in this painting, we know that in order to flourish, every living plant must be established in good soil that feeds its roots. There is the hidden strengthening that is going on beneath the ground as well as the glorious apparel of the flower itself. This is also true for prayer, where we need 'good soil': the habits and disciplines of time set aside for prayer and a sifting of words and methods so that we find the way of praying that suits us best and feeds us so that our faith blossoms and flowers. The paradox in this painting is that the 'good soil' for Jesus' praying may deliberately be a shell-hole. But this shows us that prayer can never be separate from the conflicts and sufferings of the world. In fact, it is these realities of daily life that feed our prayer as much as anything else.

Although we don't pray in order to receive energy for living in a literal sense, it is undoubtedly the case that this is the first fruits of a prayerful life. Our prayer operates in the same way. A flower is wide open: like a radar it silently follows the path of the sun across the sky. It receives the energy it needs. It is constantly replenishing. We too can be open to God. Perhaps this is what St Paul meant when he said 'Pray without ceasing' (1 Thessalonians 5.17). Live with this transparent openness to God; although for most of us – as it was for Jesus in his earthly ministry – this sort of open vulnerability to God will require the discipline of times set aside for prayer. It is only when we have ordered our life in such a way as to incorporate actual times of prayer that the whole of our life might be prayer-full.

There is one final and slightly more controversial way of looking at this picture. We know, from many of his other paintings, that Spencer's preoccupations with sex was, to say the least, unorthodox. Nevertheless, his paintings of love and sex have about them a great tenderness as well as a shocking physicality. Rarely has flesh looked so fleshly and as frail as in some of his paintings. Rarely has such desire and longing been meditated upon. Indeed, two of the chapels in his Church House were to be dedicated to his wives: his beloved first wife, Hilda, and his lover and second wife, Patricia Preece. The nude paintings of Patricia are studies in mortality, desire and an enforced restraint (Patricia Preece was a lesbian and it is likely that this doomed marriage was an almost entirely sexless affair). In one of his most famous paintings,[3] we see him nakedly squatting in quizzical adoration before Patricia's open, inviting, but untouched, naked body. In the foreground sits an uncooked leg of lamb.

In *Love Letters*, a much later painting, a young Stanley Spencer and a young Hilda squat fully clothed on the settee. Spencer holds up to his face the love letters that Hilda has written, and breathes in the fragrance of their presence. Meanwhile Hilda is pulling letters from her breast and passing them to him. It is a beautiful picture of memory and adoration and of the aroma of presence. In a letter written to Hilda in 1943, Spencer described the love letters he had received from her as being like flowers.[4]

For Spencer there was something profoundly spiritual about the intimacies of sexual union, itself becoming an image for union with God. In his paintings spirituality and sexuality are brought together. Although Spencer himself was not able to live within the disciplines of the Church's teaching on sex and marriage, in a strange way his paintings illustrate the marriage service beautifully.

This liturgy speaks of marriage as 'a gift of God in creation . . . that as a man and a woman grow together in love and trust, they shall be united with one another in heart, body and mind'.[5] It is this sort of complete union that is suggested in the painting by Jesus' powerful focus, reaching upwards to God.

The service goes on: 'The gift of marriage brings husband and wife together in the delight and tenderness of sexual union and joyful commitment'.[6] We should not be surprised, therefore, to see in this picture not just the stamen of a flower but, by association, the erect male member. There may even be a playful suggestion of this in the title of the painting itself. We shouldn't be disturbed by this. It is a vision that means that the whole of one's being is oriented towards God, that there is nothing within us that is unredeemable or outside God's purposes and desires. The whole of our life, including our sexuality, is from God and can be dedicated to God, can know God's purposes and be used for God's glory. The painting is a remarkable picture of praise, desire and union with God.

Most of us will have known such intimacy with God only in a few rare and probably fleeting moments. Hopefully we will have had moments of intimacy, either sexual or emotional or both, with other human beings, and we need to see that these unions, as the marriage service describes, are themselves a foreshadowing of the union with God that is the promise of the Christian life. Jesus embodies this union. He is the one who always rises from sleep to prayer. His whole person is directed towards God and longs to receive direction from God. As we imitate Christ, so we grow into this same pattern of praise and contemplation, asking that God's will be done in us and through us.

2

Consider the Lilies

Christ in the Wilderness: Consider the Lilies (1939)

The title of this painting tells us straight away which bit of Scripture Spencer had in front of him. From the Sermon on the Mount in Matthew's Gospel, this is a famous and well-known saying of Jesus. It follows on from his teaching on prayer. In order to begin to read the picture it is probably worth quoting the passage in full:

Therefore I tell you, do not worry about your life, what you will eat or what you will drink, or about your body, what you will wear. Is not life more than food, and the body more than clothing? Look at the birds of the air; they neither sow nor reap nor gather into barns, and yet your heavenly Father feeds them. Are you not of more value than they? And can any of you by worrying add a single hour to your span of life? And why do you worry about clothing? Consider the lilies of the field, how they grow; they neither toil nor spin, yet I tell you, even Solomon in all his glory was not clothed like one of these. But if God so clothes the grass of the field, which is alive today and tomorrow is thrown into the oven, will he not much more clothe you – you of little faith? Therefore do not worry, saying, 'What will we eat?' or 'What will we drink?' or 'What will we wear?' For it is the Gentiles who strive for all these things; and indeed your heavenly Father knows that you need all these things. But strive first for the kingdom of God and his righteousness, and all these things will be given to you as well. So do not worry about tomorrow, for tomorrow will bring worries of its own. Today's trouble is enough for today. (Matthew 6.25–34)

Jesus is speaking about God's goodness and God's provision. No one can add a moment to their life by worrying; just as the birds of the air are fed and the lilies of the field are clothed, so we will be cared for and catered for by God. Instead, we must strive for God's kingdom.

This painting plumbs the depths of this Scripture, but it does so in an upside-down kind of way. Spencer begins by subverting the text itself, for even the most cursory glance at the picture reveals that these are not lilies that Jesus is considering, but daisies! These are not the great lilies that adorn our churches on Easter morning, but the everyday flowers that grow willy-nilly in the lawn.

But before we consider the strangeness of this reversal, several other things about the picture are immediately arresting and worth noting. First, the desert itself has come to life. It is no longer a place of arid sterility. Echoing those Old Testament references to the desert blossoming and bearing fruit (see Isaiah 42.18–19), and perhaps even foreshadowing those depictions of the cross where flowers grow out of the dead wood, this desert has become a place of bountiful and lush fecundity. Jesus is surrounded by daisies. Behind him there are trees, and it also appears as if an early morning mist is being gently dispersed by the sun's first rays. This feels more like Easter Day than another day in the wilderness. Only the seed head to the immediate right of Jesus hints at death.

Jesus himself is monumental, painted like a great rock settled for all time in the heart of the landscape. Again, there are many references in Scripture to God as rock, especially in the Psalms. In Psalm 18.2, we say that God is 'my rock in whom I take refuge'. Psalm 28 begins: 'To you, O Lord, I call; my rock, do not refuse to hear me.' And Psalm 61.2 asks: 'Lead me to the rock that is higher than I.' In the New Testament, Paul picks up this imagery; remembering the story of Moses splitting the rock and water flowing forth, he says: 'they drank from the spiritual rock that followed them, and the rock was Christ' (1 Corinthians 10.4). And is it too fanciful also to remember some words of the seventeenth-century Carmelite lay brother, Lawrence, whose own deceptively simple approach to God and the presence of God in all things and every moment seems so similar to Spencer's? Describing his prayer life as simple attentiveness to God in all his creation and in all the activities of his working day, he says: 'Sometimes I think of myself as a piece of stone before its sculptor . . . setting myself thus before God, I beg him to shape his perfect image in my soul, and make me exactly like him.'[1]

But with this painting one could also make a more mundane observation: this may perhaps be the only depiction of Jesus as being fat! In fact, he is enormous, literally replete with the good things of God's good creation. This, for me, is a nice antidote to so much so-called religious art where Jesus often has a six-pack and looks as if he has just got back from the gym!

However, his rock-like grandeur is offset by the calm humility of his posture. Jesus does not command the space in a way that makes us think that we ought to bow down before him: he is monumental, but this is not a monument. On the contrary, he is down on all fours gazing in wonder at the daisies. He is at the same time huge *and* humble. And in the foreground it appears as if some of the daisies are turning their faces to him. The flowers that follow the path of the sun now strain towards Christ.

So let us ask some questions of this strange and beautiful picture. First of all, why is Jesus staring at the daisies? Is it because of all the wonderful things the daisies have achieved? No, this can't be the reason. Jesus gazes at the daisies just because they are. He delights in them for no other reason than that they are what they have been made to be. Just as Narcissus gazed in self-absorbed wonder at his own reflection, Jesus marvels at God's creation.

There is a famous passage by Thérèse of Lisieux in her autobiography, *The Story of a Soul*, where she describes her soul as being like a flower of God's garden. She writes:

The sun's light that plays upon the cedar trees, plays on each tiny flower as if it were the only one in existence; and in the same way our Lord takes a special interest in each soul, as if there were no other like it. Everything conspires for the good of each individual soul, just as the march of the seasons is designed to make the most insignificant daisy unfold its petals on the day appointed for it.[2]

And just the page before, she observes:

All the flowers [God] has made are beautiful; the rose in its glory, the lily in its whiteness, don't rob the tiny violet of its sweet smell, or the daisy of its charming simplicity. I saw that if all these lesser blooms wanted to be roses instead, nature would lose the gaiety of her springtide dress – there would be no little flowers to make a pattern over the countryside. And so with the world of souls, which is his garden. He wanted to have great Saints, to be his lilies and roses but he must have lesser Saints as well; and these lesser ones must be content to rank as daisies and violets, lying at his feet and giving pleasure to his eye like that. Perfection consists simply in doing his will, and being just what he wants us to be.[3]

I have not been able to discover whether Spencer ever read this spiritual classic, which was extremely popular in the twentieth century, but it is certainly a remarkable coincidence, for Thérèse speaks of the daisies having equal status with the lilies and of God's great love for the 'little flowers' in his garden. St Thérèse herself is, of course, known as 'The Little Flower', and is usually depicted holding a cross and a bouquet of roses. With this painting in mind, it might be better if she was holding daisies.

Can we draw the conclusion that this is how God looks at us? That we are daisies in his garden? God gazes in wonder upon the whole of his creation; he delights in it, not because of what it has achieved, but because it is. He looks at us – the souls in his garden – in the same tender and delightful way. He invites us to find satisfaction and fulfilment in being the people that we are meant to be; this is not quite saying that we must each stay in our place, but it does encourage us to grow where we have been planted, to recognize and strive for the potential that is within us, and to know that we are greatly loved as we are, as we have been made.

The other question we might ask of the picture is this: what is Jesus doing? The most profound answer is also the most obvious. Jesus is doing nothing, or at least nothing that the world would consider important, economic or productive. He is just staring at the daisies.

I have written elsewhere about 'doing nothing'.[4] In this sense, 'doing nothing' should not be viewed as wasteful idleness, but rather as contemplation. In the previous painting we looked at,

Jesus is focused entirely upon God; now he is focused entirely upon the world, and upon us. He loves the world and delights in its every detail. To rest in the presence of that which God has created is itself an act of adoration and praise.

I recall an experience many years ago when I was stopped dead in my tracks by the sight of a tiny sliver of green sprouting from some newly laid tarmac on the pavement outside my house.[5] I was so overwhelmed by the sense of nature's tenacious creativity that it was a kind of epiphany. The barren highway of the pavement was in bloom, and for a moment all I wanted to do was get down on my knees and thank God for the profligate creativity of the world. But I didn't. Even as the moment of praise arrived, it evaded my grasp. Sensible grown-upness triumphed. I didn't get down on all fours in the street. I didn't gaze in wonder at that little speck of green. I passed it by.

Jesus says that 'whoever does not receive the kingdom of God as a little child will never enter it' (Mark 10.15). In this painting we see Jesus as child, relishing the present moment, entering into its joy, doing what I was unable to do: stopping and looking. This is one of children's greatest gifts. Where we rush on to the next moment, longing to turn the next page, the child is content to dwell in the present, to savour its every possibility. So Jesus does not simply mean that to enter the kingdom we must have child-like trust in God; he means that we need to receive and enjoy life as a child, with the same qualities and attitudes of children.

And this is what we see in the picture: Jesus at play, enjoying the presence of the daisies, receiving the joys of the moment.

In fact, Spencer's original inspiration for the painting came from a memory of his daughter, Shirin, playing in the garden and regarding nature with the same innocence and wonderment that we see here in Christ. Spencer said this of the painting:

> I think I got this notion from first having made a small study of Shirin when she was a baby out on the grass, crawling about looking at the flowers. It pleased me, perhaps, more than most, I think, because it seemed to be very much more what I wanted. It seemed to be a more auspicious and possible happening and the leaning over the flowers gives me a sense of the Creator brooding over his creation, and the analogy between what a baby might do and what God might do is so near in its feeling.[6]

It may seem rather astonishing to liken God to a little toddler crawling about on the grass, but this picture, together with Spencer remembering his daughter playing in the garden, helps us to make the connection between prayerfulness and playfulness. Referring to Michelangelo's famous paintings of the creation, Spencer also notes that he was thinking of God moving upon the face of the waters. Creativity can be understood as play: God delights in the act of creating and then in the enjoyment of the creation.

Therefore there is a sense that in this picture Jesus is the great artist: not just the lover of the creation, but also the creator. And artists themselves are often, in a sense, children, or at least in touch with the child within them. They are people who have not forgotten how to play. This was especially true of Spencer. In so many of his paintings there is huge and playful delight in the most ordinary of things; and, as we observed earlier, much of his income came from his landscapes, where his great love for the countryside around Cookham and his sense of God dwelling in it shine through. Yet before the artist can draw, he must first learn to look. For it is in seeing and looking and appreciating what is, in all its unique and matter-of-fact createdness, that the artist is able to dwell with and in the subject he is re-creating.

In this respect the painting might be understood as a picture of the Sabbath, for in Scripture the Sabbath is first presented as a gift of God in creation – 'God blessed the seventh day and hallowed it' (Genesis 2.3). This is not just about rest, but about God enjoying the creation that he has made.

But the Sabbath is also a commandment – 'Remember the Sabbath day, and keep it holy' (Exodus 20.8). Our participation in the Sabbath is about our ability to become children, enjoying what is, and being set free to be co-creative with God. One of the ways we do this is by observing the creation, looking at it attentively, relishing its kaleidoscopic variety and intricacy, and seeking to behold God's presence within it. By entering fully into the joy of God's creation and our own co-creativity with God, our lives become pathways and channels of adoration.

In this picture Jesus enjoys the Sabbath rest of the moment he is in. He embodies his teaching, caring not for food or drink or clothing, but seeking God in what to us would be the most tiny and insignificant of flowers: just the daisies that we curse when they grow in our lawn, the ordinary flowers that we ignore.

For most of us, most of the time, life is very different from this. We do nothing but worry. We either rake over the past or fret anxiously about the future. Joy is something we hope for, something to purchase, an occasional treat. And because we think of it as something beyond us, to be enjoyed when we get there – a holiday, a night out, a new pair of shoes, a drink – it usually disappoints. We do not seek it in the things that are in front of us now, as a different way of dwelling in the present. We see it as a reward awaiting us in the future, something we need to earn or achieve by our own hard work. Thus, when it comes to the present moment, we're not present. If there are daisies in the lawn, we want to get rid of them. And so the painting leads us back to the Scripture with which we began, but with a shocking challenge:

> Do not worry, saying, 'What will we eat?' or 'What will we drink?' or 'What will we wear?' . . . your heavenly Father knows that you need all these things. But strive first for the kingdom of God and his righteousness,

and all these things will be given to you as well. So do not worry about tomorrow, for tomorrow will bring worries of its own. Today's trouble is enough for today. (Matthew 6.31–34)

What Spencer shows us here is the supreme vision of God's dwelling in the eternal now of his presence to us and of his great love for us. God does indeed clothe and love the lilies and the daisies. So he will also clothe and love us. What we need to do is seek his kingdom; and we need to do it with the same child-like dependency and joy that we see here in Jesus. We need to strive to dwell in the presence of the God who is forever break-ing into the 'one after another' chronology of all the separate moments that make up our lifetimes. In this we can be chal-lenged to see and delight in God in every person and in every moment itself and all that it holds. And to do this would be to dwell in heaven, to know it here on earth, to find heaven even in the most unlikely and unpromising places, even in a wilder-ness, which itself suddenly and miraculously becomes a place of fertile joy. Put simply, we are called to look upon each other in the same way that Jesus looks upon the daisies. This is what dwelling in God's kingdom looks like.

Let me give the last word of this chapter to Nadine Stair, whose oft-quoted reflections at the end of her life seem to sum up some of what this painting points to:

If I had my life to live over, I'd dare to make more mistakes next time. I'd relax, I would limber up. I would be sillier than I have been this trip. I would take fewer things seriously. I would take more chances. I would take more trips. I would climb more mountains, swim more rivers and watch more sunsets. I would do more walking and looking. I would eat more ice cream and less beans. I would perhaps have more actual troubles, but I'd have fewer imaginary ones. You see, I am one of those people who lives prophylactically and sensibly and sanely hour after hour, day after day. Oh, I've had my moments; and if I had to do it over again, I'd have more of them. In fact, I'd try to have nothing else. Just moments, one after another instead of living so many years ahead each day. I've been one of those persons who never goes anywhere without a thermometer, a hot water bottle, a raincoat and a parachute. If I had to do it again, I would go places and do things and I would travel lighter than I have. If I had my life to live over, I would start barefoot earlier in the spring and stay that way later in the fall. I would play hookey more, I wouldn't make much good grades except by accident. I would ride more merry-go-rounds. I would pick more daisies.[7]

3

The Scorpion

Christ in the Wilderness: The Scorpion (1939)

At first sight this picture could not present a greater contrast to *Consider the Lilies*. A mournful, wretched and weary-looking Jesus squats in the desolate wastelands of a desert that is once again a place of stark emptiness. Nothing grows. The sky is as bleak and colourless as the landscape. In his hands Jesus cradles a scorpion. Another one scuttles at his feet.

Although the venom of most scorpions is not dangerous to human beings, some species are deadly, and this is an animal we rightly fear. In all countries where scorpions are found they are treated with respect and suspicion. They are to be either avoided or eliminated. In her prose poem 'Scorpion', Jo Shapcott writes about this primeval fear of scorpions – and much else besides. Finding a scorpion in the room, the protagonist of the poem beats it to a pulp with her shoe. Each line of the poem begins with the words, 'I kill it'.[1]

In the picture the feared scorpion shares centre stage with Christ. As with some of the other paintings in this series, it is not immediately clear which Scriptures Spencer is drawing on. However, a little investigation reaps a shocking reward, and the fear of the scorpion is at the heart of it. Scorpions are mentioned twice in the Gospels, both times in Luke.

Jesus says, 'Is there anyone among you who, if your child asks for a fish, will give a snake instead of a fish? Or if the child asks for an egg, will give a scorpion?' (Luke 11.11–12). This is Luke's version of the more well-known saying in Matthew: 'Is there anyone among you who, if your child asks for bread, will give a stone?' (Matthew 7.9). Again we find Spencer subverting a familiar text: the bewildering implication of this picture is that it is God the Father who will give such a thing to his Son. It is Jesus who holds the scorpion in his hands.

While none of Spencer's pictures draws precisely on the actual stories of Jesus in the desert, this one comes closest. Each of the synoptic Gospels describes the desert as a place of temptation. Matthew's and Luke's accounts include details of the temptations themselves. Jesus fasts for 40 days. He is famished. Then the devil comes to try and ensnare him. First, Jesus is invited to turn stones into bread; then to launch himself from the pinnacle of the Temple and have the angels save him; finally, to receive all the kingdoms of the world if he will but bow down before the devil. Jesus responds: life is more than bread, we also feed on every word that comes from God; this God must not be put to the test; we must worship God alone (see Matthew 4.1–11; Luke 4.1–12).

Jesus holding the scorpion is also a temptation. It is not what he has asked for. He has resisted turning the stones to bread, but he still longs for food. He is hungry; instead there are stones at his feet. He longs for an egg or a fish. Instead he is given a scorpion. He is asked to receive the thing he fears, the thing that could kill him.

This painting takes us from the temptations in the desert to the crisis of Gethsemane, the place where Jesus, again in great anguish and desperation, cries out to God that there might be another way: 'Father, if you are willing, remove this cup from me' (Luke 22.42).

Jesus wants there to be another way. He searches his own conscience and he pleads with God. It is a crisis of vocation. Jesus has resisted the temptations of the devil in the wilderness, but now finds himself faced with the last and greatest temptation of all: he could turn his back on what he has come to realize is his calling, which is to be the one who, as it were, receives the scorpion, fulfils the Father's will, surrenders himself to the sufferings that will quickly follow – if he does not escape now.

The second mention of scorpions in Luke is when the 70 return joyfully from the preaching mission Jesus has sent them on. They say to Jesus: 'Even the demons submit to us!' (Luke 10.17). Jesus replies: 'I watched Satan fall from heaven like a flash of lightning. See, I have given you authority to tread on snakes and scorpions, and over all the power of the enemy; and nothing will hurt you' (Luke 10.18–19).

But in the picture, Jesus relinquishes the power that he has observed in those who follow him. Instead Jesus displays another sort of power. He does not subdue the scorpion. He does not tread it underfoot. He loves it. Jesus receives and holds and cherishes the very thing that could kill him. He has arrived at a point of complete acceptance of God's will. His focused intimacy with God bears fruit in this utter self-surrender of himself to the worst that the world has to offer. 'Not my will but yours be done,' says Jesus (Luke 22.42). Thus, he looks upon the scorpion with the same tender longing with which he beheld the daisies. 'There is extraordinary gentleness in the way Christ holds the scorpion and looks at it, an infinite pity,' says Richard Harries.[2] And again: 'In the face of Christ . . . there is an unutterable gentleness and compassion.'[3]

In many respects this picture is the shadow of the one we looked at in the previous chapter. The daisies and the scorpions are two sides of one coin. The ability to love one must include the ability to love the other. Jesus says:

> You have heard that it was said, 'You shall love your neighbour and hate your enemy.' But I say to you, Love your enemies and pray for those who persecute you, so that you may be children of your Father in heaven; for he makes his sun rise on the evil and on the good, and sends rain on the righteous and on the unrighteous. (Matthew 5.43–45)

The Christian vocation is to love unreservedly and unconditionally. Its hallmark is the love of enemy: love of that which is inexplicable and dangerous. It is easy to love those who love you, says Jesus (see Matthew 5.46), but here is an altogether different sort of love.

As well as Gethsemane, this is therefore a picture of the cross. It is where Jesus' reconciliation to the Father's will leads. In Gethsemane Jesus prays, 'If it is possible, let this cup pass from me' (Matthew 26.39). On the cross Jesus cries out, 'I thirst' (John 19.28), which refers not just to the exhausting agony of his Passion, but to his longing to do God's will, to be the one that he is called to be. He longs to take the cup the Father gives and drain it to the dregs.[4] 'Your will be done' becomes the driving energy of his Passion. Indeed, John's account, which does not include the agony in the garden of Gethsemane, begins with Jesus uttering these words as he is arrested: 'Am I not to drink the cup that the Father has given me?' (John 18.11). In the language of this painting Jesus is saying: 'Am I not to receive the scorpion the Father gives me?'

In his death upon the cross Jesus walks the second mile that he bids all his followers travel (Matthew 5.41). He goes on loving: not just those who love him, but his enemies, even those who now conspire to crush him. He doesn't fight back. God's will is in him transparently. He is silent before his accusers. Taking to himself all those ancient and never really understood prophecies, he becomes the lamb that before its shearers is silent (see

Isaiah 53.7). He does not judge. He loves those who persecute him. He takes the mocking and the scoffing. He does not answer back. He tells those who hammer in the nails that they are forgiven (Luke 23.34). He reaches out in hopeful, confident reassurance to the thief who hangs alongside him (Luke 23.43). He loves the scorpion.

The composition of the painting is exquisite. Each detail is an essay. Jesus elects not to tread on the scorpion that brushes past his feet. He holds the other scorpion in his hands. He looks at it tenderly. He has learned how to love his enemy. He is showing us what it looks like. His fingers are swollen. It might be fanciful to say that they look a little like the plaited loaf of bread he longs for: and the bread of life that he has become. There is a more obvious interpretation, which is the right one. The reason his fingers are swollen is because he has been stung. Stung, and he goes on loving, goes on holding the scorpion.

Notice how Spencer has painted Jesus' hands in precisely the position in which we hold them when we receive Holy Communion. For that is what this picture is about: a complex holding together of Gethsemane and Calvary; temptation and reconciliation; Jesus' struggle to be reconciled to God's will, and his wonderful and astonishing acceptance of that will; his surrender and offering of himself. It is a picture of communion: Jesus' complete communion with the Father's will, and his making possible of our communion, through him, with God. He will indeed become the bread of life. And our sharing in this bread will be our communion with God.

Henri Nouwen tells a moving story about an old man and a scorpion. An old man sees a scorpion trapped on a root in a fast-flowing river, unable to free itself. The man reaches out to save the scorpion, but every time his hand comes near the scorpion it stings him. 'You stupid old man,' says a passer-by. 'Don't you know that the scorpion will kill you?' 'Why be angry because I am generous?' replies the man. 'It is in the scorpion's nature to sting. It is in my nature to save.'[5]

Thus we see Jesus, not carrying the cross, not nailed to it, but squatting in the desert holding the scorpion that can kill him, doing what it is in his nature to do; for as God's Son he comes to perfectly fulfil God's will, to be the suffering servant who reconciles us to God, and to do for us what we could never do for ourselves.

The clouds behind Jesus suggest the gloom of gathering darkness. In the Gospels the whole Passion of Christ happens during the night or in darkness. As Judas goes out to betray Jesus, John observes, 'It was night' (John 13.30). The trial before the Sanhedrin is in the night. As Jesus dies on the cross, darkness covers the earth (Mark 15.33). Even at the resurrection, Mary Magdalene goes to the tomb 'while it was still dark' (John 20.1). The sense of approaching darkness in the painting leads us to this strange gospel truth, that God does his greatest deeds in darkness and unknowing. Indeed, Christ's Passion and death are an encounter with the darkness of the world.

Christ's body is positioned almost as if he is giving birth (poor Middle Eastern women would often squat when in labour). And of course this is one of the meanings of Christ's Passion and death: it is a birth, a re-creation. Out of the darkness a new light dawns.

In the climactic eighth chapter of his letter to the Church in Rome, Paul declares that 'the sufferings of this present time are not worth comparing with the glory that is about to be revealed to us' (Romans 8.18). He speaks of the whole creation waiting with 'eager longing for the revealing of the children of God' (Romans 8.20); that 'the creation itself will be set free from its bondage to decay and will obtain the freedom of the glory of the children of God' (Romans 8.22). Taking up the theme of labour and birth, he goes on:

> We know that the whole creation has been groaning in labour pains until now; and not only the creation, but we ourselves, who have the first fruits of the Spirit, groan inwardly while we wait for adoption, the redemption of our bodies. For in hope we were saved. (Romans 8.22–24)

It is the labour pains of the new creation that we see in Jesus as he holds the scorpion. By his wounds we have been healed. We see him patiently waiting, patiently suffering, hoping for the things that cannot yet be seen (see Romans 8.25).

4

The Foxes Have Holes

Christ in the Wilderness: The Foxes Have Holes (1939)

One of the Sunday supplements I read regularly publishes each week a feature on some celebrity or other, and in each interview the celebrity is asked the same questions. As I read the pieces I sometimes find myself wondering what I would say if I was asked this particular set of questions. One of them is this: what is your favourite journey?

Now this is a fascinating question. And in more than one of life's idle moments I too have found myself thinking about some of my favourite journeys. Let me tell you about a few of them. I used to love the journey up the M1 to Yorkshire – coming off at Junction 38 and driving across the Pennines to Huddersfield, seeing Castle Hill appear on the horizon, and then the sight of that most handsome of West Yorkshire towns nestling in the natural amphitheatre of the Colne Valley. Learning the lesson of the daisies, I would even sometimes stop, get out of the car and drink in the beauty of that moment. And I love the A1 just as much – particularly leaving the road and driving towards Peterborough, and catching the first glimpse of Peterborough Cathedral. It is especially beautiful at night, when the cathedral is floodlit, and sits upon the flat horizon of the fens like a great ship. And I have come to love the M4 – east or west, but especially Junction 12, where the road takes you through Theale and then back over the motorway and up towards the Thames. Latterly I have developed a similar affection for the M25 and the A12, particularly the stretch from Junction 28 up towards Chelmsford. It is exceedingly beautiful: a journey of uninterrupted delight.

As for great train journeys, is there anything to match the Trans-Pennine Express? Or Paddington to Reading? Or, best of all, Fenchurch Street to Southend-on-Sea? As the train leaves London behind it hugs the banks of the Thames, offering striking and expansive views across the estuary towards Kent – they would never be allowed to get away with building it today. When the sun is high and the tide is out the mud flats look mysteriously beautiful, holding the shape of a million rippling waves in the up-turned palms of their hands. Fishing smacks lean on their hulls, resting. Fishermen mend nets. People walk their dogs. It is a wonderful sight. The train rushes along, and stretched out on either side is the satisfaction of landscape and people at ease, in their place.

My favourite journey doesn't take me all the way to Southend. I get out of the train at Leigh. I breathe in the salt air. It is the place where I am happy to stop.

Why are these my favourite journeys? Perhaps you've guessed – these are my journeys home. For nine years I lived in Huddersfield, but my work took me all over the country and I seemed to be forever driving up and down the M1; and it was fantastic when I caught the first sight of home. Likewise Peterborough and Reading, and now Chelmsford. And Leigh-on-Sea is the place where I was born and brought up. Its views across the Thames estuary, its little fishing boats; everything about it speaks to me of home and belonging.

By contrast, this picture of Jesus shows him without a home. It is a picture of longing, a yearning for a reality that cannot yet be seen. He has a home, but it is not here. He longs to rest; but he cannot rest here.

Spencer has placed Jesus in some sort of wood. It appears to be winter; the colours are grey-green and a sombre yellowish red. This is a lifeless desert. There is nothing green. We see trees, but they are hardly living, just roots and the base of trunks. The two trees behind him appear to have calcified, as if they have been blighted by some poisonous rain. 'It is a sort of "placeless" place,' says Spencer. 'You are in a sort of nowhere and nowhere is not home, and this making a double home – one for the foxes and one for Christ – brings about a homely feeling that I want without altering anything else in Nature.'[1]

A lost, haggard and hungry-looking Jesus has stopped and is leaning against some sort of bank. In the foreground a fox pops its head out of a hole to look at him. Either side of him other foxes go in and out of their holes.

The verses of Scripture that Spencer begins with are these: someone comes up to Jesus and says that he will follow him wherever he goes. In Luke's account we are not told who this person is; in Matthew it is a scribe: that is, someone already identified as a God-seeking person. Jesus replies: 'Foxes have holes, and birds of the air have nests; but the Son of Man has nowhere to lay his head' (Matthew 8.20; Luke 9.58). Jesus is saying that while birds in their nests and foxes in their holes – and by implication all the animals of the world, we human beings included – have their homes here on earth, he has no such place. Therefore, all who follow him will be accompanying him in this restless, homeless wandering.

Someone then says, 'Lord, first let me go and bury my father.' He is prepared to follow Jesus, but has other things to attend to first. Jesus replies: 'Follow me, and let the dead bury their own dead' (Matthew 8.21–22; Luke 9.59–60). In Luke's account Jesus also adds that the person must 'go and proclaim the kingdom of God' (Luke 9.60). Another person wants to say goodbye to his loved ones first. Jesus rebukes him as well: 'No one who puts a hand to the plough and looks back is fit for the kingdom of God' (Luke 9.61–62).

The scriptural message seems clear, and at first sight Spencer's depiction of it appears obvious: my home is not of this world, the picture seems to be saying; the Son of Man has a home that is beyond the homes of the world. Jesus' hard words of rebuke to those who want to bury loved ones, or say goodbye to families, also speak of a discipleship that is demanding and all-consuming. To follow Jesus seems to mean going with him into the unknown. It means being without a home and without loved ones. This is undoubtedly the demanding implication of what Jesus is saying, and though it will not be everyone's vocation to take such a sacrificial path of discipleship, this is what it means for some of us; and all of us who follow Christ must arrive at a place of readiness, where following him may incur leaving everything else behind. But, beautifully, Spencer's painting has added some other layers of meaning to this difficult saying.

Notice how the careful composition of the painting places the holes in which the foxes live in exact symmetry with the billowing, open sleeves of Jesus' robes. Is there another message here? At the same time as having no home on earth, this symmetry shows Jesus perfectly assimilated to the earth. This would have been very important for Spencer; in all these pictures he wants to show Jesus' ease with and love for nature. And there are important ecological conclusions for us. We rarely live in such harmony with our surroundings. Nevertheless, Jesus is in the world completely and yet at the same time not of the world: part of it and yet looking and longing for something beyond it.

His temptations in the desert are leading him to a place of exacting knowledge. He is coming to discern God's very particular call on his life. He is to be the one who perfectly fulfils God's purposes in the world and for the world. He is going to demonstrate God's great love for the world. He will restore a lost relationship with God, and will do this by treading the difficult path of suffering love. He is leading the world to its true home. Therefore, much though he loves the world – and goodness knows, Spencer's pictures, not least *Consider the Lilies*, where Jesus delights in the daisies, show how God loves the world that he has made – he must take us through it to the new creation, the great biblical promise of a new heaven and a new earth, where God himself will be temple, light and life, where tears will be wiped away and where restless yearning will cease.

Spencer apparently emphasized this joyfully on his deathbed in 1960. Preaching at the memorial service for him at St James's, Piccadilly on 27 January 1960, the Revd M. Westropp, Vicar of Cookham at the time and a friend of Stanley's, said: 'He told my wife that dying and reaching heaven would be a sense of relief of being safe again, of being home, of being where one belongs.'[2]

Jesus' continuity with the landscape, his looking restlessly beyond it, and the prompt of the text itself, illustrate brilliantly Spencer's love of the world and his longing for what is beyond it in heaven. This is further emphasized by the fact that the foxes – notoriously timid animals, especially with humans – are so at ease in the presence of Christ.

Every human knows that life is a journey, and that the life we enjoy now will come to an end. This is not a specifically religious concept. You don't need to be a Christian to know this. Life begins when we are born. It ends when we die. As we get older, we become aware that there is more road behind us than what is left up ahead of us. All human beings shudder as the shadow of impending death creeps upon us. We not only fear the pain of dying, but the horror of not being, the utter emptiness of not having all that we now enjoy. Little wonder that we often respond by putting down deep roots in this life itself. We know that those roots cannot sustain us for ever. And in our own culture, where we hardly talk about death at all, we imply that when it comes it is some sort of tragedy or failure. Well, of course it is a tragic loss for the person involved, and for their family and loved ones, but it is only what we know will happen one day. It is something every one of us will have to do eventually. Neither courage, exercise, diet, nor prayer can prevent it. Science may continue to achieve ever more astonishing things: limbs may be regrown, corpses might one day be resuscitated. But in the end – ultimately – death will win. There will even be a day when the whole universe collapses back upon itself. It is all just a matter of time – and of the end of time itself.

The Christian story embraces death. It is not an ending; it is not a tragedy. Jesus' death on the cross shows God's involvement with the world he loves, even with its suffering and death. Through the resurrection we see a new beginning – a first sighting of that new creation. And now we look at the painting again and begin to wonder whether Jesus' posture might suggest something else?

His arms are spread out. The shape and shadow of the cross are already upon him.

The death of Jesus is a doorway through which we travel. Life, which had seemed like a journey going nowhere, one that ended in the nothingness of death, now becomes a holy pilgrimage, a journey home. The biblical vision tells us that in the city of God there will be no temple, 'for its temple is the Lord God Almighty and the Lamb', and it has 'no need of sun or moon to shine on it, for the glory of God is its light, and its lamp is the Lamb' (Revelation 21.22–23). So, in this picture, Jesus himself may not yet have a home, but there is an invitation for us to find our home in him; and through his cross we have a home with God. The foxes have their holes in the bank. We have the swelling, open sleeves of Jesus' garment. There is room for us there. Our home is Christ. Heaven is a person as much as a place. In following him, we can still, like him, be at home in the world, but never entirely at peace: our home with him will take us to another home that is beyond this life. The trajectory of our lives will be redirected.

There is one further detail to observe. Look at Jesus' hands. His right hand is open and his left hand is clenched. His right hand is strong and healthy: it mirrors the tail of the fox beneath it. His left hand appears dead: it mirrors the cold, apparent deadness of the tree trunk above it. Jesus carries both life and death within himself. He carries openness to God so that we might be open. He carries clenched closed-ness that it might be prised open.

Life and death are in him, so that our lives and our deaths might be in him as well.

And we mustn't miss the obvious.[3] Jesus is in a foxhole – like the foxholes Spencer would have known in Salonika when he worked as an ambulance driver and then as an infantryman. As an old soldier once remarked: 'There are no atheists in a foxhole.'

5

The Hen

Christy in the Wilderness: The Hen (1954)

A couple of summers ago I was on holiday with my family in the Languedoc, a hot, rugged and beautiful region of southern France. We had rented a small house for a couple of weeks, and most days we met up with other members of my extended family who were staying nearby. We spent a lot of time by the river: much less crowded than the beaches and lovely to swim in.

At the end of the holiday, having to vacate the house early and also wanting to make the most of the last day, we packed our car and headed for the river as usual. As we all sat in the car ready to set off I suddenly burst into tears. In that moment I realized that family life as I had known it for the past 18 years was about to end. My eldest son was off to university, and the other two were growing up; this might be the last day of the last family holiday we would have like this. Even if there were more holidays together (and there have been), they would be different – not just with girlfriends coming along too, but once one leaves home, even for university, life is never quite the same again. Family life adjusts, and moves on; young people grow up and build lives of their own. It is what should happen. But it is painful in that one sudden moment which defines itself as a turning point, an ending and a beginning. Sitting in the car, knowing that this was an ending, and with them gathered around me, I cried for joy that I had been given the fantastic privilege of being a father and having a family, and also with sadness that they were growing up, moving on, going their own way.

As I write this, other memories of family togetherness come back to me. I remember a summer's evening some years ago while we were living in Berkshire, when we walked up into Sulham woods. It had been a hot day and in the cool of the evening we set off towards the woods, about a half-hour walk. But while we were walking through the woods, under the canopy of the trees, there was a sudden torrential downpour of rain. We huddled together at the foot of the largest tree we could find and gathered branches around us and sat out the passing storm as best we could. There was a wonderful magical togetherness under the tree. The rain beat down. We held on to each other, joking and telling stories.

When the children were even smaller I remember how every day started with a cuddle. One by one, right up until they were almost teenagers, each of them would come into our bed in the morning and all five of us would lie there holding each other, jostling for position and waiting for the day to begin. I can recall my own childhood: memories of Sunday lunch with all of us round the dinner table, or in the car off on holidays ourselves. I hold all these memories in my heart; I cherish them.

In her poem '7301', U. A. Fanthorpe reflects on 20 years of joyous, fulfilling relationship. The number 7301 refers to the number of days she and her partner have spent together, and she reckons that with a bit of luck they may have another 7301 in front of them. She describes it as 'colossal crops of shining tomorrows'[1] crammed in her arms. As it turned out, she was about right: she died about 20 years after writing this poem. She and her partner were still together. The poem celebrates the shared memories of love. Its optimism and joy are infectious. But it is also doomed. The days do come to an end. We try to hang on to them for as long as possible. But eventually they run out.

This picture of Jesus encircling the mother hen, who is herself gathering together and encircling her chicks, is an image of this desire to hold things together for as long as possible, and to protect those we love. Notice the cockerels patrolling (or is it prowling?) outside the circle of Christ's embrace. This desire to gather and protect is natural. It depicts a longing that is deep inside every human being, and especially every parent. As I discovered, sitting in the car that day, my children with me, this is something I will always long for: to know that they are together, safe with me, that we are one family.

As mentioned earlier, not all of us will have enjoyed the intimate togetherness of family life that was my childhood experience and, I hope, that of my children. Indeed, some people have horrific experiences of family life. But even the successful family must be left behind. In fact, that is the aim of parenting. It is the foundation upon which other lives are built. But it is also the scaffolding. Once the building is erected, the scaffolding is removed and put away, and although there are times when I wish I could go back and have those days again, I know that life isn't like this. Life moves forward. That is the message of the foxes and their holes. We are at home and not at home. We belong in the world, but our true home is beyond it.

But what is it moving towards? Encircling the protective refuge of the mother hen is Christ himself. He is the protecting presence around all the temporary homes that we erect. And the haven of the mother hen is safe. The little chicks are drawn to the security of her care. So our homes and our places of refuge, and the love and security we have with each other, are real. But around them is the greater reality that is God. It is from God that all these things had their being in the first place; it is to God they will eventually travel. This is the presence of Christ, through whom the world was made: 'He is the firstborn of all creation, for in him all things in heaven and on earth were created' (Colossians 1.15). But Paul goes on: 'In him all things hold together' (Colossians 1.17). That is what we see in this picture: Christ holding things together. And he is also the one in whom we will find our final rest: 'Through him God was pleased to reconcile to himself all things, whether on earth or in heaven' (Colossians 1.20). He is our end.

The promise of the Christian faith is a promise of restoration: a time when all the scattered fragments of our lives are gathered into a place of safety and refuge, just like the longing we have to draw our own loved ones together and to hold them close. It is also a present reality. What God promises at the end can also be enjoyed and experienced now, through our fellowship with Christ. He is the one who cares for us and protects us, watches out for us and longs to gather us together.

The image of the mother bird protecting her offspring under the shadow of her wing captures this perfectly. It is an image that crops up a lot in Scripture, particularly the Psalms. 'Hide me under the shadow of your wing,' says Psalm 17.8. 'In the shadow of your wings I will take refuge, until the destroying storms pass by,' begins Psalm 57. The image comes from an observation of nature, but in these psalms it is directly related to God. 'Thus,' says Walter Brueggemann, 'the metaphor [of the protecting wing] embodies openness to a new purpose, a submission to the will of another, a complete reliance upon the protective concern of another.'[2]

The other paintings in this series were completed during the first few years of the Second World War, most of them in 1939. But this one was painted much later, in 1954. It is not surprising, therefore, that it has a slightly different feel. The wilderness is not blooming, but neither is it wild or forbidding. The landscape behind Jesus is homely and gentle. He could even be on the beach. The very presence of the hen and its chicks suggests a domestic setting.

The biblical text that Spencer is working from is easy to identify. In Matthew's and Luke's Gospels Jesus cries out:

> Jerusalem, Jerusalem, the city that kills the prophets and stones those who are sent to it! How often have I desired to gather your children together as a hen gathers her brood under her wings, and you were not willing! See, your house is left to you, desolate. For I tell you, you will not see me again until you say, 'Blessed is the one who comes in the name of the Lord.' (Matthew 23.37–39; Luke 13.34–35)

But comparing the accounts, he says this at two slightly different times. In Luke Jesus says this *before* he enters Jerusalem. His words foreshadow the shouts of triumph that the people will cry out when he comes towards the city, riding on a donkey, entering it as Messiah. They do indeed shout out joyfully, 'Blessed is the king who comes in the name of the Lord! Peace in heaven, and glory in the highest heaven!' (Luke 19.38). And even when some of the Pharisees in the crowd try to stop them, Jesus responds: 'I tell you, if these were silent, the stones would shout out' (Luke 19.40). As the city itself comes into view Jesus weeps over it, saying: 'If you, even you, had only recognized on this day the things that make for peace! But now they are hidden from your eyes' (Luke 19.42).

In Matthew he says these words in Holy Week itself: that is, *after* he has entered into Jerusalem and after the crowds have shouted, 'Hosanna . . . Blessed is the one that comes in the name of the Lord' (Matthew 21.9). If they are to say these words again they must, therefore, point to another coming.

The words are therefore spoken directly to God's chosen people Israel, and Jesus says them as he enters, or as he looks forward to entering, Jerusalem. He comes as the one promised by God, whose sacred task it is to gather all people together in himself and, in the words of the letter to the Ephesians, 'create in himself one new humanity . . . thus making peace' (Ephesians 2.15). But he recognizes the great cost of this vocation. Jerusalem is the place that kills or stones those who are sent to it. He says these words knowing that he has turned his face against the temptations of the devil to rule over the kingdoms of the world. Instead he comes to the holy city in order to gather the kingdoms of the world into the kingdom of God.

There is great desire in his heart: a maternal desire to gather a family together. Jesus has become the embodiment of the God who is the eternal loving parent. He is himself the Mother Hen, who wants only to protect and gather together her brood. Hence Spencer paints Jesus as a Mother, both pensive and protecting. In one sense he is resting at last: this is a picture of where we are going, the final fulfilment, an eternal gathering together; but it is also thoughtful – there are other hens outside of his enveloping care. At the same time he is anxious – perhaps there is still danger abroad. Jesus recognizes that some will not be willing to be drawn into the circle of his care. Some will attack him. Others will abandon him. Eventually he will die alone. But it is for a purpose, so that all can be gathered together. This is his heart's desire. It is the desire of God.

Maternal images for God are rare in Scripture, and even in the Church today, but Spencer has chosen to show one in this picture. But just because this idea is not often put into words does not mean that it is not true: God is both Father and Mother, and these words of Jesus witness to God's maternal nature. Implicit in Scripture, though as I say, rarely expounded, the idea of Jesus as Mother was famously taken up by St Anselm in the eleventh century and Mother Julian in the fourteenth. Quotations by both of these writers, in modern versions of their originals, can be found set as canticles in *Common Worship*. Anselm, Archbishop of Canterbury at the very end of the eleventh century and one of the Church's very greatest theologians, says: 'Jesus, like a mother you gather your people to you; you are gentle with us as a mother with her children.'[3] Mother Julian, an English anchorite and mystic, writing in her *Revelations of Divine Love*, or *Shewings*, as the old English has it (by the way, this immensely significant book is probably the first ever written in English by a woman), says: 'God chose to be our mother in all things'; that just as 'our mothers bear us for pain and for death; our true mother, Jesus, bears us for joy and endless life'.[4] And Brother Lawrence, whose simple spirituality has never been far from us throughout this book, writes in a letter to his confessor:

My commonest attitude is this simple attentiveness, an habitual, loving turning of my eyes to God, to whom I often find myself bound with more happiness and gratification than that which a babe enjoys clinging to its nurse's breast. So, if I dare use this expression, I should be glad to describe this condition as the 'breasts of God', for the inexpressible happiness I savour and experience there.[5]

Spencer chooses this text, with all its motherly connotations, for what turned out to be the last of his Christ in the Wilderness paintings. The 40 he dreamed of were never to come into being, yet those that were completed give us a startling insight into Jesus' vocation and self-understanding of his ministry. They show his great love for the earth, for the whole created order and for all creatures within it. They lead us to a profound reflection on what it means to follow Jesus, and to be people of prayer; to be people who gaze at daisies and cradle scorpions; to be people who, like the foxes in their holes, find their home in Christ; and who, like the mother hen who gathers her chicks together, are ourselves gathered into the safe embrace of a God who is Mother and Father to us all, and who longs to gather the whole creation into a new creation.

Like all great art, the paintings speak to us at various different levels and pose just as many questions as they answer. But they lead us deeply into the grace-filled mystery of Christ's own relationship with the earth, his relationship with God and his relationship with us. Here, truth is not found in an index. It cannot be neatly extracted. You can't just blithely ask: what do these paintings mean? You have to dwell with them, live with them, let them lead you into the wilderness.

For Christians this wilderness is a place of discovery. For Spencer it is a place where life can be put in proper kilter and perspective. By dwelling in the wilderness of these paintings we can refine our own discipleship. We can learn again what it means to follow Christ. We can learn to be Christ-like in our attitudes to others and to the world. We can reach out to him afresh – for we are the daisies he loves, the scorpions he holds, the foxes that have their homes in him, and the chicks he longs to gather under his wing.

The circle is not completely closed. In the foreground, between Jesus' left arm and his feet, one little chick is coming in to land. There remains an opening through which more can enter. There will always be a place for those who can see Jesus and cry out those words of recognition: that Jesus is the 'Blessed One, who comes in the name of the Lord'.

In the end, that was all that happened to the so-called penitent thief on the cross. It was not contrition that he offered to Jesus but recognition (see Luke 23.39–43). 'Remember me in that kingdom of yours,' is what he cried out, but it was enough. That is still true today. Following Jesus at a distance is OK. Following tentatively is OK.

In John's Gospel Jesus says, 'I am the gate. Whoever enters by me will be saved, and will come in and go out and find pasture' (John 10.9). But in this densely beautiful passage, Jesus also says that he is the Good Shepherd (John 10.14). He has come to bring abundant life (John 10.10). He is the shepherd and the gate and the promise of life. All this is wonderfully gathered together in Spencer's image. There is reassurance and there is promise. In this picture Jesus is both the sheepfold where safe pasture can be found – the Good Shepherd who loves and envelops the hen and its chicks: 'I know my own and my own know me' (John 10.14) – and the gate through which one enters.

Look again and you will see that the little bird coming in to land isn't a chick at all. It is something else – a sparrow, a welcome cuckoo in the chickens' nest. 'I have others that are not of this fold and I must bring them in also,' says Jesus.' They will listen to my voice. So there will be one flock, one shepherd' (John 10.16). All this, and so much more. There is room for everyone. The spaciousness of the desert is matched by the spacious, abundant love of Spencer's all-embracing Christ.

Afterword

Contemplation and desire –
reading the art and spirituality of
Stanley Spencer

In the Introduction I mentioned my art teacher, Rosemary Murray, showing me a copy of Stanley Spencer's painting *Swan Upping at Cookham*. This is one of his earliest works and it helped establish him as an artist when he was starting out. Seeing this picture for the first time was also the beginning of my love for and interest in Spencer's paintings.

Begun in 1915 and then abandoned during his wartime service (it was finished in 1919), it is the first of Spencer's mature paintings which also depict his spiritual experiences and intentions. Immersing himself back in the life of the village after the war, he started to see the everyday life and activities of the village as sacred, as revealing the presence and the purposes of God. He also developed the view – partly as a way of coping with the traumas of war – that in the eyes of God, all work was of equal importance.[1]

George Herbert famously wrote:

> Teach me, my God and King,
> in all things thee to see;
> and what I do in anything
> to do it as for thee.[2]

The title of this poem (now so well known as a hymn) is 'The Elixir', the fabled philosopher's stone that alchemists believed could turn anything into gold. Herbert applies the concept to everyday life, to 'drudgery made divine'. This, he says, is the 'famous stone' which 'turneth all to gold'. And alongside Herbert are other similar sources of Christian wisdom.

The French Jesuit Jean-Pierre de Caussade (1675–1751) writes, in his book *The Sacrament of the Present Moment*:

> The present moment holds infinite riches beyond your wildest dreams but you will only enjoy them to the extent of your faith and love. The more a soul loves, the more it longs, the more it hopes, the more it finds. The will of God is manifest in each moment, an immense ocean which only the heart fathoms insofar as it overflows with faith, trust and love.[3]

Also in the seventeenth century, Brother Lawrence served as a lay brother in a Carmelite monastery in Paris. Most of his life was spent working in the kitchens, and in old age repairing sandals. Yet his serenity and his intimacy with God meant that he was much sought after as a spiritual guide. It was said of him that the 'good Brother found God everywhere, as much while he was repairing shoes as while he was praying'.[4] After his death, his writings were collected together and compiled into the classic Christian text known as the *Practice of the Presence of God*. In it he says:

> People look for ways of learning how to love God. They hope to attain it by I know not how many different

practices. They take much trouble to abide in his presence by varied means. Is it not a shorter and more direct way to do everything for the love of God, to make use of all the tasks one's lot in life demands to show him that we love, and to maintain his presence within by the communion of our heart with his? There is nothing complicated about it. One only has to turn to it honestly and simply.[5]

For Brother Lawrence, 'common business', no matter how mundane or routine, could be a medium of God's love. The sacredness or worldly status of a task mattered less than the motivation behind it:

> The time of action does not differ from that of prayer. I possess God as peacefully in the bustle of my kitchen, where sometimes several people are asking me for different things at the same time, as I do upon my knees before the Holy Sacrament. My faith even becomes so enlightened that I think I have lost it. It seems to me that the curtain of obscurity is drawn, and that the endless cloudless day of the other life is dawning.[6]

And returning to his common theme, he says:

> It is not needful to have great things to do. I turn my little omelette in the pan for the love of God. When it is finished, if I have nothing to do, I prostrate myself on the ground and worship my God, who gave me the grace to

make it, after which I arise happier than a king. When I can do nothing else, it is enough to have picked up a straw for the love of God.[7]

This sort of spirituality – the sense of the presence of God in all things and the possibility of honouring God in every action – is evident in the paintings, and indeed the writings, of Stanley Spencer. Shaped by this spirituality, small events like swans being carried up the High Street in wheelbarrows on wing-clipping day became, in Spencer's language, 'doorsteps' in which spiritual significance and pleasure could be found in the living out of everyday life.

On one occasion he was in church on a Sunday morning when he heard punts being launched up the river at Turk's boatyard – the place depicted in this painting of swan upping – and he wrote in his diary:

> The village seemed as much a part of the atmosphere prevalent in the church as the most holy part of the church such as the altar . . . And so when I thought of people going on the river at the moment my mind's imagination of it seemed . . . to be an expression of the church atmosphere.[8]

For Spencer too, the curtain of obscurity is drawn; the endless cloudless day of the other life begins to dawn. He even refers to Cookham as a 'village in heaven', and this is the title of a painting of the village he completed in 1937. It is not shown as a comfortable rural idyll, but bursts with joyful energy as people are drawn into communion with each other.

Thinking back to his time working in hospital, he wrote: 'I did not despise any job I was set to do, and did not mind doing anything so long as I could recognize in it some sort of integral connection with the spiritual meaning that demanded to be clarified.' In this we know that he was quite directly influenced by some words of St Augustine. In 1915 Spencer was working as an orderly at the Beaufort hospital in Bristol, and he made friends with a young Roman Catholic, Desmond Chute. Desmond introduced him to St Augustine's *Confessions*, where he found these words: that God was 'ever busy, yet ever at rest – gathering, yet never needing, bearing, filling, guarding, creating, nourishing, perfecting'. This validated his delight in the cosy domesticity of the everyday and lifted the doing of a menial task to an expansive spiritual plain. This attitude is most poignantly illustrated in his wartime paintings in the Sandham Memorial Chapel at Burghclere, where the same soldiers who on the east wall are seen resurrected are, on the panels either side, depicted picking bilberries, making beds and cleaning tea urns.

In 1934 Spencer was asked to contribute to a series of essays called *Sermons by Artists*. What he writes sums up so much of the spirituality that shaped the paintings that this book has explored. Increasingly, the motivation for his paintings was to capture (and at the same time release and explore) the presence of God in the world around him, especially the people and places that he loved most, and also to retell the story of Christ through his own story and in his own village. Because he was writing a sermon he had a text. His choice is revealing: 'He that loveth not, knoweth not God, for God is love' (1 John 4.8, AV).

In the sermon he writes: 'The instinct of Moses to take his shoes off when he saw the burning bush was very similar to my feelings. I saw many burning bushes in Cookham. I observed this sacred quality in most unexpected places.'[9] And later on: 'After steeping myself in the Bible I began to realize certain things which gave me a greater capacity to love until I was able to see things equally inspiring to love outside the Bible.'[10]

It is impossible to understand and appreciate Stanley Spencer's art without knowing something of his faith. His faith was not straightforward (whose is!), but he loved the Bible, the Church, and most of all he loved Christ. His paintings are iconic, in the literal sense of that word: windows into God, or, as Spencer alludes, places of encounter, burning bushes. Consequently, each of the paintings we have looked at in this book is a burning bush: a place of vivid encounter with God. They lead us to stillness, to contemplation, to a greater appreciation of God's presence, and an increased desire to know Christ and follow in his way.

Notes

Introduction: Stanley Spencer and me

1 The Sandham Memorial Chapel, Harts Lane, Burghclere, near Newbury, RG20 9JT; tel: 01635 278394; email: <sandham@nationaltrust.org.uk>; website: <www.nationaltrust.org.uk/sandham-memorial-chapel/>.

2 Stanley Spencer Gallery, High Street, Cookham, Berks SL6 9SJ; tel: 01628 471885; email: <info@stanleyspencer.org.uk>; website: <www.stanleyspencer.org.uk>.

3 Jane Alison, 'The Apotheosis of Love', in *Stanley Spencer: The Apotheosis of Love*, Exhibition Catalogue, Barbican Art Gallery, 1991, p. 1.

4 Alexandra Harris, *Romantic Moderns: English Writers, Artists and the Imagination from Virginia Woolf to John Piper*, Thames & Hudson, 2010.

5 Kenneth Pople, *Stanley Spencer: A Biography*, Collins, 1991, p. 399.

6 Pople, *Stanley Spencer*, p. 513.

7 Stanley Spencer's reflections on the Christ in the Wilderness series, dictated to his niece Daphne in 1950, and obtained from the archivist of the Stanley Spencer Gallery in Cookham.

8 Spencer's reflections.

9 Quoted in Fiona MacCarthy, *Stanley Spencer: An English Vision*, Yale University Press, 1997, p. 104.

10 Spencer's reflections.

11 Pople, *Stanley Spencer*, p. 399.

12 Tate Archive, quoted in Pople, *Stanley Spencer*, p. 399.

13 Richard Harries, in his unpublished notes on these paintings.

14 Spencer's reflections.

15 Rowan Williams, 'The Wisdom of the Desert', *Retreats*, No. 191, The Retreat Association, 2011, p. 10.

16 Williams, 'The Wisdom of the Desert', p. 10.

1 Rising from Sleep in the Morning

1 Stanley Spencer's reflections on the Christ in the Wilderness series, dictated to his niece Daphne in 1950, and obtained from the archivist of the Stanley Spencer Gallery in Cookham.

2 Spencer's reflections.

3 This painting, *Double Nude Portrait: The Artist and his Second Wife*, finished in 1937, a couple of years before the Christ in the Wilderness paintings were begun, can be seen in the Tate collection.

4 'My soul will as before in that room go out into the unknown hours stretched before it & flower & flower & buds will come anywhere, in a pocket, or from my pencil & from my pocket will come love letters to you & I will see you open that one flower & the pencil opens others. Revealing my thoughts.' From the Tate Gallery Archive, 733.2, and quoted in Jane Alison, 'The Apotheosis of Love', in *Stanley Spencer: The Apotheosis of Love*, Exhibition Catalogue, Barbican Art Gallery, 1991, p. 88.

5 The Marriage Service, *Common Worship: Pastoral Services*, Church House Publishing, 2000, p. 105.

6 The Marriage Service, p. 105.

2 Consider the Lilies

1 Brother Lawrence, *The Practice of the Presence of God*, translated by E. M. Blaiklock, Hodder & Stoughton, 1981, p. 31.

2 Thérèse of Lisieux, *The Story of a Soul*, translated by Ronald Knox, Fontana Books, 1958, p. 27.

3 Thérèse of Lisieux, *The Story of a Soul*, p. 26.

4 See Stephen Cottrell, *Do Nothing to Change Your Life*, Church House Publishing, 2007.

5 Described in Cottrell, *Do Nothing to Change Your Life*, p. 55.

6 Stanley Spencer's reflections on the Christ in the Wilderness series, dictated to his niece Daphne in 1950, and obtained from the archivist of the Stanley Spencer Gallery in Cookham.

7 The internet will give you many versions of these words, attributed to Nadine Stair and said to have been written when she was 85. It is not known where they first appeared, though it may have been the *Reader's Digest*, October 1953 issue, where they were attributed to Don Herold (1889–1966), author and humorist. I came across them in the journal *Ministry Today*.

3 The Scorpion

1 Jo Shapcott, 'Scorpion', in *Of Mutability*, Faber & Faber, 2010, p. 13.
2 Richard Harries, in his unpublished notes on these paintings.
3 Richard Harries, sermon preached at Cookham Parish Church, 30 June 1991, the 100th anniversary of Stanley Spencer's birth.
4 For a longer discussion of this interpretation of Jesus' words in John's Gospel see my book *I Thirst, The Cross – The Great Triumph of Love*, Zondervan, 2003, especially Chapters 3 and 4.
5 Henri Nouwen, *Seeds of Hope*, Darton, Longman & Todd, 1989, pp. 124–5.

4 The Foxes Have Holes

1 Stanley Spencer's reflections on the Christ in the Wilderness series, dictated to his niece Daphne in 1950, and obtained from the archivist of the Stanley Spencer Gallery in Cookham.
2 The Revd M. Westropp, sermon preached at memorial service for Stanley Spencer, 27 January 1960, St James's, Piccadilly, Stanley Spencer Gallery Archive.
3 For some of these observations I am indebted to participants on the Saffron Walden Team Ministry Parish Weekend in May 2011. They helped me see new things, in this picture in particular.

5 The Hen

1 U. A. Fanthorpe, '7301', in *A Watching Brief*, Peterloo Poets, 1987, p. 33.
2 Walter Brueggemann, *Praying the Psalms: Engaging Scripture and the Life of the Spirit*, Paternoster, 2007, p. 38.

3 Anselm of Canterbury, 'A Song of Anselm', *Common Worship: Daily Prayer*, Church House Publishing, 2005, p. 639.

4 Julian of Norwich, 'A Song of Julian of Norwich', *Common Worship: Daily Prayer*, Church House Publishing, 2005, p. 643.

5 Brother Lawrence, *The Practice of the Presence of God*, translated by E. M. Blaiklock, Hodder & Stoughton, 1981, p. 31.

Afterword: Contemplation and desire

1 For a further discussion of the development in Spencer's painting see Keith Bell, *Stanley Spencer*, Phaidon Press, 1992, p. 35.

2 George Herbert, 'The Elixir', in *George Herbert: Country Parson, The Temple*, edited by John Wall, SPCK, 1981, p. 311.

3 Jean-Pierre de Caussade, *The Sacrament of the Present Moment*, first published in France, 1966, English translation Collins, 1981.

4 Brother Lawrence, *The Practice of the Presence of God*, translated by E. M. Blaiklock, Hodder & Stoughton, 1981, p. 81.

5 Brother Lawrence, *The Practice of the Presence of God*, p. 79.

6 Brother Lawrence, *The Practice of the Presence of God*, p. 78.

7 Brother Lawrence, *The Practice of the Presence of God*, p. 78.

8 Quoted in A. Causey, 'Stanley Spencer and the Art of His Time', in *Stanley Spencer RA*. Exhibition catalogue, Royal Academy of Arts, 1980, p. 23.

9 *Sermons by Artists*, Golden Cockerel Press, 1934, p. 50.

10 *Sermons by Artists*, p. 51.